Jupiter

OUR SOLAR SYSTEM

Mary Kurkalang

PICTURE CREDITS

Cover: Jupiter © Photolibrary.

Page 1, Photolibrary; page 4, Photodisc; page 5 (top) ©
Photolibrary; page 5 (bottom), Photo Essentials; page 6,
Photolibrary; page 7 (top) © Myron Jay Dorf/Corbis/Tranz; page
7 (bottom) © eStock Photo/Alamy; page 8 © Photolibrary;
page 9, Risteski Zitiste/BigStockPhoto.com; pages 11–12 ©
Photolibrary; page 13 © Corbis/Tranz; page 14, Photolibrary; page
15 © courtesy Space Science Institute/JPL/NASA; page 19 ©
Photolibrary; page 21 © Louie Psihoyos/Corbis/Tranz; page 22
(middle), Photodisc; page 22 (bottom) © Archivo Iconografico,
S.A./Corbis/Tranz; page 23 (left) © Bettmann/Corbis/Tranz; page
23 (right), Digital Vision; page 24 © courtesy NASA, ESA, and The
Hubble Heritage Team (STScI/AURA); page 25 (left), Photodisc;
page 25 (right) © Photolibrary; page 26 © Photolibrary; page 29,
Photodisc.

Produced through the worldwide resources of the National
Geographic Society, John M. Fahey, Jr., President and Chief
Executive Officer; Gilbert M. Grosvenor, Chairman of the Board.

PREPARED BY NATIONAL GEOGRAPHIC SCHOOL PUBLISHING
Sheron Long, Chief Executive Officer; Samuel Gesumaria,
President; Steve Mico, Executive Vice President and Publisher;
Francis Downey, Editor in Chief; Richard Easby, Editorial Manager;
Margaret Sidlosky, Director of Design and Illustrations; Jim Hiscott,
Design Manager; Cynthia Olson and Ruth Ann Thompson, Art
Directors; Matt Wascavage, Director of Publishing Services; Lisa
Pergolizzi, Production Manager.

MANUFACTURING AND QUALITY CONTROL
Christopher A. Liedel, Chief Financial Officer; Phillip L. Schlosser,
Vice President; Clifton M. Brown III, Director.

EDITOR
Mary Anne Wengel

PROGRAM CONSULTANTS
Dr. Shirley V. Dickson, National Literacy Consultant; James A.
Shymansky, E. Desmond Lee Professor of Science Education,
University of Missouri-St Louis.

National Geographic Theme Sets program developed by Macmillan
Education Australia Pty Limited.

Published by the National Geographic Society
1145 17th Street N.W.
Washington, D.C. 20036-4688

ISBN: 978-1-4263-5167-9

Product# 4P1005174

Printed in Hong Kong.

2011 2010 2009 2008 2007
1 2 3 4 5 6 7 8 9 10 11 12 13 14 15

Contents

Our Solar System

A star and the objects that move around it make up a solar system. These moving objects include planets, asteroids, comets, and moons. There are millions of solar systems in the universe. The sun is the star at the center of our solar system. Earth is a planet that moves around the sun. Other planets move around the sun too. Four of these planets are Mercury, Mars, Jupiter, and Saturn.

Key Concepts ··

1. The sun is a star at the center of our solar system.
2. Our solar system contains planets, asteroids, comets, and moons.
3. Planets in our solar system have different features.

Four Planets in Our Solar System

Mercury

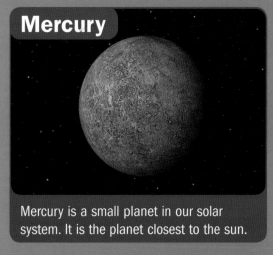

Mercury is a small planet in our solar system. It is the planet closest to the sun.

Mars

Mars is a rocky planet in our solar system. It appears red in color.

In this book you will learn about the planet Jupiter in our solar system.

Jupiter

Jupiter is the largest planet in our solar system. It is made up of gases.

Saturn

Saturn is a large planet in our solar system. It has rings around it.

Jupiter

Imagine you are a space traveler. You can travel anywhere you want in our solar system. Your journey takes you past many planets. Some are larger than Earth and some are smaller. You see moons circling the planets. At the center of our solar system is the sun. The sun is the largest object in our solar system. All the other objects, including the planets, move around the sun. Jupiter is one of the planets. It is the largest planet in our solar system.

 Key Concept 1 The sun is a star at the center of our solar system.

The Solar System

Each **solar system** has a star at its center. Other objects **revolve** around the star. The sun is the star at the center of our solar system. Jupiter and seven other **planets** revolve around the sun. Each planet moves in a fixed path called an **orbit.**

solar system
a group of objects that revolves around a star

Jupiter

A force called **gravity** holds planets and other objects in their orbits around the sun. A large group of stars is called a **galaxy.** A galaxy can contain billions of stars and all the objects that revolve around the stars. Galaxies also contain dust and gases. The sun is just one of over 200 billion stars in a galaxy called the Milky Way.

The spiral-shaped Milky Way galaxy

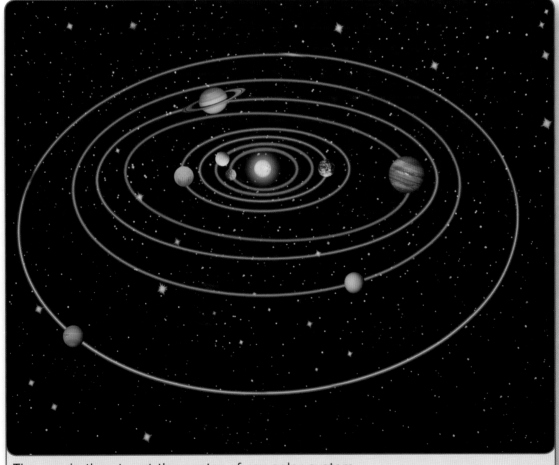
The sun is the star at the center of our solar system.

How the Sun Formed Scientists think that the sun, like all stars, formed from a cloud of dust and gas called a **nebula.** Stars go through stages as they form. Each stage takes millions of years. First, gravity makes the nebula shrink. When the nebula shrinks enough, the dust and gas are pulled together to form a star. The star begins to give off heat and light energy.

What the Sun Is Like The sun is a ball of gases that produce heat and light energy. Hydrogen and helium are the two most common gases in the sun. The outer layer of the sun gives off heat and light energy. This is the layer you can see from Earth. The temperature in the outer layer of the sun is about 6,000° Celsius (11,000° Fahrenheit).

Why the Sun Is Important The sun is important because the heat and light energy it gives off keeps animals and plants alive on Earth. Without the sun's heat and light, nothing could survive on Earth.

Layers of the Sun

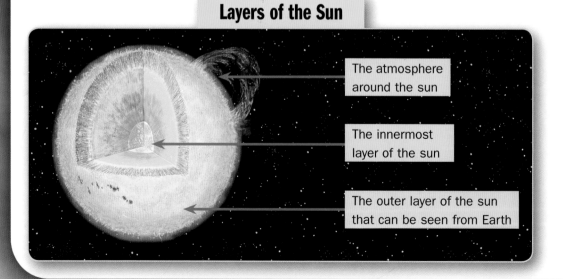

The atmosphere around the sun

The innermost layer of the sun

The outer layer of the sun that can be seen from Earth

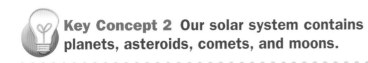
The Planets

Our solar system contains eight planets that revolve around the sun. The planets are Mercury, Venus, Earth, Mars, Jupiter, Saturn, Uranus, and Neptune.

Inner and Outer Planets Scientists place the planets into two groups—the Inner Planets and the Outer Planets. The Inner Planets are closer to the sun. They are alike in many ways. They are all smaller than most Outer Planets, and they have rocky surfaces. However, Inner Planets also differ. Mercury is a lot hotter than Earth because it is closer to the sun. Earth is the only Inner Planet that has water and oxygen.

All Outer Planets are big. They are mostly made of gases. Some Outer Planets have rings around them that are made of rock, ice, or dust.

Inner and Outer Planets

9

How Planets Move Like Earth, all planets move in two ways. First, they spin, or rotate, on an **axis.** An axis is an imaginary line that runs through a planet's two poles. Second, planets revolve around the sun in their orbits. Some planets take longer than others to rotate or revolve once. It takes Earth 24 hours, or one day, to rotate once on its axis. It takes Earth 365 days, or one year, to revolve once around the sun.

Earth's axis is tilted. This tilt causes seasons. In June, July, and August, the Northern Hemisphere is tilted toward the sun. The Northern Hemisphere gets more heat and light energy in those months. It is summer here. At this time of year the Southern Hemisphere is tilted away from the sun. It is winter here.

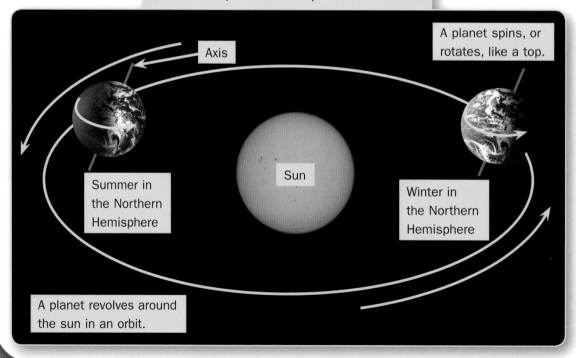

Rotation, Revolution, and Seasons

Axis

A planet spins, or rotates, like a top.

Sun

Summer in the Northern Hemisphere

Winter in the Northern Hemisphere

A planet revolves around the sun in an orbit.

Asteroids

Asteroids are pieces of rock and metal that revolve around the sun. Scientists think that asteroids may be parts of planets that did not form properly, or broke up. Asteroids are of different sizes. The largest known asteroid is about 960 kilometers (596 miles) wide.

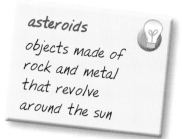

asteroids
objects made of rock and metal that revolve around the sun

Because asteroids are so far from Earth, you can see them only through a telescope. There are thousands of asteroids in our solar system. Most are found in an area known as the asteroid belt. This belt falls between the planets Mars and Jupiter.

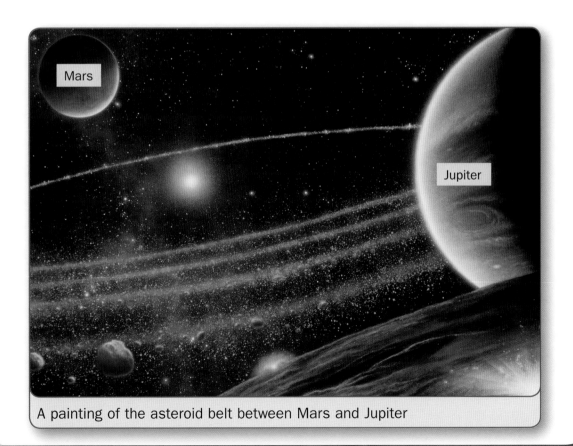

Mars

Jupiter

A painting of the asteroid belt between Mars and Jupiter

Comets

Comets are chunks of rock, ice, gas, and dust. This material was most likely left over from when the planets formed.

Like planets and asteroids, comets revolve around the sun in their orbits. Sometimes, a comet's orbit can be a giant oval path. When a comet's orbit brings it close to the sun, the sun's heat melts some of the ice. The ice becomes gas. The gas then mixes with dust to form a long tail. Comets can have tails that are up to 100,000 kilometers (62,000 miles) long. Some tails are so bright they can be seen from Earth.

Comet Hale-Bopp was first noticed in 1995. Its blue tail is made of glowing gas. Its white tail is made of dust particles.

Moons

Moons are objects that revolve around planets or asteroids. Scientists have identified more than 130 moons in our solar system. All the planets, except Mercury and Venus, have moons revolving around them. Earth has one moon and Mars has two. Jupiter has at least 63 moons that have been identified so far.

Moons can be different sizes, but a moon is always smaller than the planet it revolves around. The largest moon in our solar system is Ganymede. It revolves around Jupiter. Ganymede is larger than the planet Mercury. The smallest moon, Deimos, belongs to Mars.

Moons are not all made of the same material. Moons close to the sun are made mostly of rock and dust. Moons farther away from the sun are made mostly of ice. Earth's moon is rocky, dusty, and dry.

Jupiter and three of its moons

Jupiter

Jupiter is the largest planet in our solar system. It is the fifth planet from the sun and the first of the Outer Planets. Jupiter has at least 63 moons. Scientists continue to find more moons.

Jupiter's **diameter** is about 143,000 kilometers (89,000 miles). This is more than 11 times the diameter of Earth. Jupiter is one-tenth the size of the sun. As well as being the largest planet, Jupiter is also the heaviest planet. Its **mass** is 318 times greater than the mass of Earth.

When you look at Jupiter through a telescope, you see a large, red spot on its surface. Scientists call this the Great Red Spot. The Great Red Spot is a huge storm that has been raging on Jupiter for hundreds of years.

Earth

Jupiter

Formation and Physical Features Jupiter, like the other Outer Planets, formed far from the sun. Scientists think that Jupiter may have a solid rock **core.** The core is surrounded by layers of gases and other materials that form an **atmosphere.** The atmosphere appears like colored bands of thick clouds that are white, yellow, brown, and red. The light-colored bands are called zones. The dark-colored bands are called belts.

Belt

Zone

Belt

Jupiter's atmosphere is made of colored zones and belts.

Scientists call Jupiter a gas giant. This is because it is huge and mostly made of gases. Jupiter has three rings around its equator. Scientists think these rings are made mostly of dust.

Temperature Because Jupiter is farther away from the sun, it is much colder than Earth. However, Jupiter's temperature can vary greatly. High in Jupiter's atmosphere, it is cold. The temperature here is about -140° Celsius (-220° Fahrenheit). Closer to the core, it is hot. The temperature here is about 24,000° Celsius (43,000° Fahrenheit). This is hotter than the surface of the sun.

Orbit and Rotation Jupiter revolves around the sun in an elliptical orbit. Its orbit is longer than Earth's because it is farther away from the sun. It takes Earth one year to complete one orbit of the sun. It takes Jupiter more than 11 Earth years to complete one orbit of the sun.

Jupiter barely tilts toward or away from the sun while it revolves. This means it does not have seasons like Earth does. Seasons are caused by a tilt in a planet's axis. The side of the planet that tilts toward the sun is warm. The side that tilts away is cool.

Jupiter rotates faster than any other planet. It takes just under 10 Earth hours for Jupiter to rotate once on its axis. It takes Earth 24 hours to rotate once on its axis.

Orbits Around the Sun

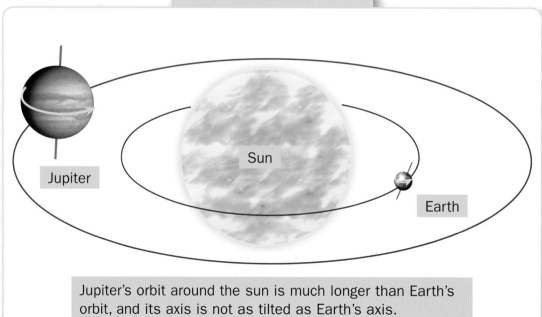

Jupiter's orbit around the sun is much longer than Earth's orbit, and its axis is not as tilted as Earth's axis.

Think About the Key Concepts

Think about what you read. Think about the pictures and diagrams. Use these to answer the questions. Share what you think with others.

1. How was the sun formed?

2. What objects are part of our solar system?

3. What is the difference between *rotate* and *revolve*?

4. What are the physical features of the planet you have learned about?

Cross-Section Diagram

Diagrams are pictures that show information.
You can learn new ideas without having to read a lot.
Diagrams use pictures and a few words to explain ideas.

There are different kinds of diagrams.
The diagram of Jupiter on page 19 is a cross-section
diagram. A cross-section diagram shows the inside of
something. It shows what something looks like if you cut
a section out of it. Look back at the cross-section diagram
on page 8. It is a cross-section diagram of the sun.

How to Read a Diagram

1. **Read the title.**
   It tells you what the diagram is about.

2. **Read the labels and captions.**
   They tell you about the parts of the diagram.

3. **Study the picture.**
   The picture shows how the parts fit together.
   This diagram shows the inside of Jupiter.

4. **Think about what you learned.**
   Decide what new information you learned from
   the diagram.

Cross-Section of Jupiter

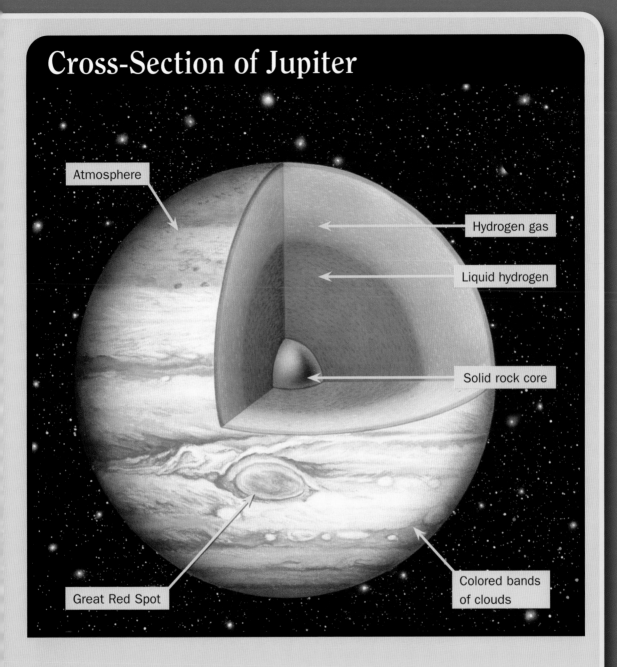

Atmosphere

Hydrogen gas

Liquid hydrogen

Solid rock core

Great Red Spot

Colored bands of clouds

What's Inside?

Read the diagram by following the steps on page 18. Write down all the things you learned about Jupiter. Share what you learned with a classmate. Compare what you learned. What is the same? What is different?

Feature Article

A **feature article** gives interesting information about a topic. Feature articles are usually written for magazines or newspapers. They often give readers detailed information in an entertaining way. The feature article starting on page 21 is about telescopes.

A feature article usually includes the following:

The **lead** draws readers in and makes them want to keep reading. For example, the lead may be a startling fact or an interesting question.

Subheads break the article down into easy-to-identify sections.

Body paragraphs give information relating to each subhead.

Photographs and **illustrations** show interesting images related to the topic.

The **conclusion** may summarize the article. It may also tell a final fact, give a final quote, or make a prediction about the future.

Telescopes

Windows to Our Solar System

Since ancient times, people have looked at the sky in wonder. They have told stories about the tiny dots of light in the night sky. They have linked the stars and the patterns they make with gods and goddesses. Most of all, people have been amazed at the sheer number of stars in the sky.

New stars form all the time. Many stars are too faint to be seen. But imagine being able to see these stars up close. Imagine learning facts about the stars that are real and more amazing than those described in stories!

The **title** tells what the topic is about.

The **lead** captures the reader's attention.

Photographs and **illustrations** show images related to the topic.

Captions tell what a picture is about.

A telescope magnifies objects to many times their size.

The First Telescope

Subheads break the article into sections.

Body paragraphs give details related to the subhead.

One day in the 1400s in Holland, two children of a spectacle-maker were playing with two glass lenses. They put the lenses together and then looked through them at a distant church tower. They were amazed at what they saw. The tower looked closer. The spectacle-maker then put a number of lenses together. This invention was called a spyglass. The military first used the spyglass to spy on enemies.

An Italian scientist, Galileo Galilei, invented the first telescope in 1609. His telescope changed what people knew about space. For example, people thought the moon had a smooth surface. Galileo's telescope showed that it had craters and peaks. Galileo used his telescope to see other things for the first time. He saw the moons of Jupiter and the rings of Saturn. His telescope could magnify objects up to 30 times their size.

Spectacles

Galileo Galilei demonstrating his telescope

Reflecting Telescopes

In 1704, an English scientist, Sir Isaac Newton, invented a new telescope. Instead of lenses, he used a curved mirror. The mirror could gather light and reflect it back. The bigger the mirror, the more light it could gather. More light helped Newton see farther.

Over time, scientists built larger telescopes with bigger mirrors. In 1929, a scientist named Edwin Hubble began looking through a giant telescope. He observed galaxies located beyond the Milky Way.

A Telescope in Space

Telescopes located on Earth cannot always give a clear view of objects in space. Clouds and dust in Earth's atmosphere make the view unclear. A telescope in space, above Earth's atmosphere, gives a clearer view.

In 1977, the United States began building a space telescope. The project took eight years to complete. It cost nearly 2.2 billion dollars. The new telescope was called the *Hubble Space Telescope*, or simply *Hubble*. It was named after Edwin Hubble.

Isaac Newton and his telescope

Hubble Space Telescope

Amazing Views from Hubble

Hubble was launched into space in 1990. It now revolves around Earth far above clouds that block the view from Earth. The *Hubble* telescope is unmanned. No astronauts travel with *Hubble*.

Scientists operate *Hubble* by remote control from Earth. These scientists are located at a space flight center in the United States. Scientists at the center keep track of *Hubble* and the information it sends back.

Hubble is a very large telescope. It is almost as long as a large school bus. It is 13.2 meters (43.5 feet) long and weighs 11,110 kilograms (24,500 pounds). *Hubble* has a long tube, open at one end, with mirrors that reflect light and cameras that take pictures.

An image of a cloud of dust and gases in space, taken by *Hubble*

Hubble circles Earth every 97 minutes. So far, it has traveled over 4.8 billion kilometers (3 billion miles). Every day, it sends data back to Earth. Thanks to *Hubble*, we have seen thousands of stars and galaxies in space. These pictures help scientists understand the universe.

Hubble has helped measure the distance between stars. From the data sent by *Hubble*, scientists know how fast stars move and how fast the universe is expanding.

Hubble has helped us understand our own solar system. It has taken amazing pictures of Mars, Pluto, and Jupiter. It has also sent back pictures of events in space. When the comet Shoemaker-Levy 9 collided with Jupiter in 1994, *Hubble* captured clear images of the collision. This helped scientists understand what happens when objects in space collide.

An image of the Eagle Nebula, taken by *Hubble*

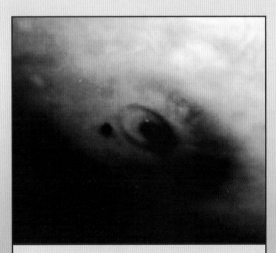

This dark spot surrounded by rings is where the comet Shoemaker-Levy 9 collided with Jupiter.

Hubble's Future

Hubble is now old. Some of its parts need to be repaired or replaced. Only two of the instruments used to hold the telescope steady and point it in the right direction are working. *Hubble's* solar batteries are losing their power. Sending astronauts to repair *Hubble* is very risky. Scientists may send a robot up to do the repair work.

In the meantime, a replacement for *Hubble* is being built. It is called the *James Webb Space Telescope*. The new telescope will be ready in 2011. It will be even more powerful than *Hubble*.

When *Hubble* is replaced, it will be brought back to Earth. Perhaps *Hubble* will be put in a museum. After all, it has helped people better understand space.

The **conclusion** may summarize the article or give a final thought or prediction.

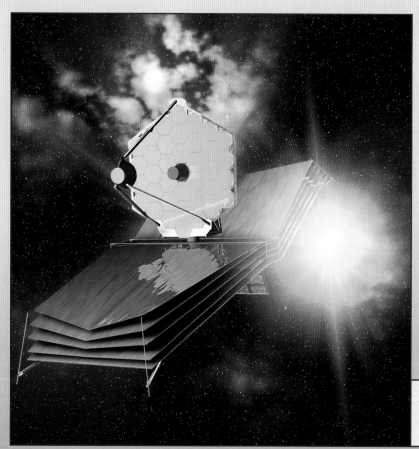

A painting of the *James Webb Space Telescope*

Apply the **Key Concepts**

Key Concept 1 The sun is a star at the center of our solar system.

Activity

Think about the different facts you know about the sun. How large is it? What is it made of? How is it important to Earth? Draw a concept web showing what you know about the sun.

Key Concept 2 Our solar system contains planets, asteroids, comets, and moons.

Activity

Imagine you are an astronaut. You are traveling around our solar system. What different objects can you see from the window of your spacecraft? Write a few paragraphs describing what you see in space.

I can see . . .

Key Concept 3 Planets in our solar system have different features.

Activity

Choose one Inner Planet and one Outer Planet. Compare the distance of the planets from the sun, their temperatures, the time it takes for them to complete one orbit of the sun, and whether or not they have seasons. Present your findings in a chart.

	Mars	Jupiter
Distance		
Temperature		
Orbit		
Seasons		

Write Your Own Feature Article

A feature article is written to give interesting information to the readers of a magazine or newspaper.

1. Study the Model

Look back at the description of a feature article on page 20. Then reread the article on pages 21–26. Look for examples in the text that make this a good feature article. How does the lead help focus the article? How do the subheads make the topic clearer? What interesting information is included? Look at the pictures again. Think about how they help make the topic interesting.

Writing a Feature Article

- Use a title that identifies the topic.
- Write a lead that interests readers and makes them want to continue reading.
- Include interesting facts.
- Use subheads to organize your facts.
- Write a conclusion that ties ideas together.

2. Choose Your Topic

Now choose one feature of space that you would like to find out more about. Think about what type of reader your article might have. Will you be writing for someone who is interested in planets and the solar system, or someone who is interested in space exploration? Once you have chosen your topic and audience, you are ready to start.

3. Research Your Topic

Make a list of questions you need to answer when writing your article. Remember that you want to focus on interesting facts about the topic. Think about what your reader might like to know. Now use the library or Internet to get your facts.

4. Take Notes

Take notes on what you find out. Look for ways to organize your information. One way to do this is to list the subheads you plan to include. Put each piece of information you find under the subhead it fits with.

5. Write a Draft

Look through your list of facts and subheads. Do they tell you something interesting about your topic? If they do, begin your draft. Start with a lead that grabs the reader's attention. If you need to, reread page 20 to recall the other important parts of a feature article.

6. Revise and Edit

Reread your draft. Does it have all the elements of a feature article? Does the organization make sense?

Exploring the Moon

1. How do people travel to the moon?

2. Who was the first person on the moon?

3. When did this happen?

Present Your Feature Article

Now you can share your work. Get together with others to make a class magazine. Follow the steps listed below.

How to Make a Magazine

1. Check that each article has a title.
The title should name the topic.

2. Include photographs or pictures for each article.
Use photographs or draw pictures to illustrate the articles.

3. Add captions to pictures.
Remember, captions tell what pictures are about.

4. Decide on the order of the articles and number the pages.
Add a page number to each page.

5. Prepare a table of contents.
Examine the table of contents in this and other books.
Now make one for your magazine.

6. Make a cover.
Talk with your group about what you want on your cover.
Choose pictures that show what is inside the magazine.
Then make your cover.

7. Now bind the pages together.
You can staple the pages together. Or you can punch holes on the left side and tie the pages together with yarn.

Glossary

asteroids – objects made of rock and metal that revolve around the sun

atmosphere – layers of gases that surround objects in space

axis – a line through the center of a spinning object

comets – chunks of rock, ice, gas, and dust that revolve around the sun

core – the center of an object

diameter – the distance across the center of a circle, or a sphere

elliptical – oval in shape

galaxy – a large cluster of stars, gases, and dust in space

gravity – a force that pulls one object toward another object

mass – the amount of matter in an object

nebula – a cloud of dust particles and gases in space

orbit – the path taken by an object moving around another object

planets – large objects that revolve around a star in an orbit

revolve – to move around an object in a fixed path

solar system – a group of objects that revolves around a star

Index